WORLD FAITHS
ISLAM

In this book, CE stands for
Common Era and BCE for
Before Common Era, with the
Common Era beginning in the year 0

The publishers would like to thank the following editorial
consultant for his help:
Dr M.A.Zaki Badawi, Principal, The Muslim College, London

First published in 2005 by Kingfisher
This edition published in 2013 by Kingfisher
an imprint of Macmillan Children's Books
a division of Macmillan Publishers Limited
20 New Wharf Road, London N1 9RR
Basingstoke and Oxford
Associated companies around the world
www.panmacmillan.com

ISBN 978 0 7534 3508 3

This edition copyright © Macmillan Publishers Ltd 2005

Material in this edition previously published by Kingfisher Publications in
The Kingfisher Book of Religions in 1999

1 3 5 7 9 8 6 4 2
1TR/1112/UTD/WKT/128MA

A CIP catalogue record for this book is available from the British Library

Printed in China

ISLAM

Worship, festivals and ceremonies from around the world

TREVOR BARNES

KINGFISHER

CONTENTS

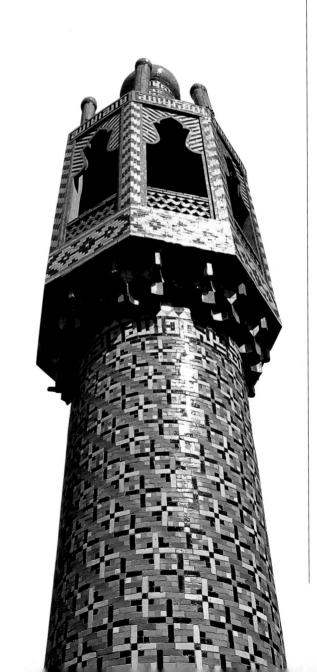

INTRODUCTION

I slam, which is translated as 'submission to God', is the religion practised by Muslims, who number around a thousand million worldwide. It is based on the teaching of the Prophet Muhammad, who is believed to have received the revealed word of Allah (God) some 1,400 years ago, in what is now Saudi Arabia.

The final revelation

Muslims believe that aspects of the divine message to humanity were also revealed to the prophets of the past (including Moses and Jesus), but that Muhammad was the last of the prophets to bring Allah's final message to the world. The message is contained in the Koran, Islam's holy book, which cannot be changed or added to. Such is the reverence for Muhammad that whenever the faithful speak his name they respectfully say after it, 'peace be upon him'.

It is said that the message of Allah was revealed to Muhammad by the chief angel Jibril, or Gabriel. Christians believe that Gabriel, who the Koran also records, appeared to the Virgin Mary to foretell Jesus' birth. The revelations of Jibril were given over a period of years and brought together in the Koran, which is central to Muslim life. This is believed to contain a complete system of belief and practice binding on Muslims everywhere.

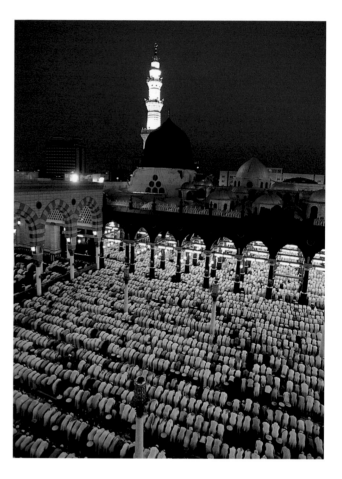

Above Muslims submit themselves to the will of God by prostrating themselves in worship. They can pray alone or, as here, with their fellow Muslims in a public display of devotion that is very impressive.

A way of life

Islam is a whole way of life with guidelines for the moral, legal, spiritual and political organization of society. In Islam nothing is regarded as secular (non-religious) and every action or thought should be guided by complete submission to the will of Allah. Indeed, Muslims are described as slaves to Allah and servants to their fellow human beings.

Left The hilal, or crescent moon and star, is the symbol of Islam. In the Koran it says that Allah created the stars to guide people to their destination. The moon is a reminder that the Islamic year is governed by the lunar calendar.

Above This 16th-century Persian engraving shows pupils studying the Holy Book at the feet of their teacher.

Below Children are expected to study the Koran and to be able to recite large parts of it by heart.

A revolutionary message

Islam emerged at a time when Judaism, Christianity and polytheism (worship of many gods) existed alongside each other on the Arabian peninsula. Many worshipped idols, so Muhammad's revolutionary message of the 'One Creator God' was upsetting and people rejected it. And yet, within 30 years, Islam became a powerful religion and later the basis of an influential Islamic empire. Islam teaches that Allah the Merciful will judge all our actions when we die. If we have done what is good and lawful (*halal*) we will be rewarded with eternity in heaven; if we have done what is not permitted (*haram*) we will go to hell. Islam is sometimes misunderstood in the West and the term 'Muslim fundamentalist' is frequently used as an insult. It is also misleading – all Muslims take their faith very seriously, so it is natural for them to follow fundamental principles. An increasingly secular West sometimes finds such devotion hard to understand.

THE DEVELOPMENT OF ISLAM

Islam developed first in Mecca, the birthplace of the Prophet Muhammad, and later in Medina. Mecca was situated on one of the principal trade routes in the Middle East, a location that may have helped Islam to be 'exported' throughout the world.

Above The influence of local architectural styles can be seen in this mosque in Mali, west Africa. The mosque is made of mud.

Early beginnings

At first Islam was no more than a localized sect of a few believers led by a man who believed Allah was revealing His message to him. This belief brought Muhammad and his followers into conflict with the merchants of Mecca, who did not want an important (and profitable) place of pilgrimage for Arab pagan beliefs threatened by the message that there was only One God. Muhammad and his followers were persecuted and eventually forced to leave. They moved north to Yathrib (later named Medina) in a migration that became known as the *hijra*. It marks the beginning of Islam as an organized religion.

Medina

At Medina, the Prophet Muhammad continued to receive divine revelations, among them rules of law that he applied to the growing community of Muslim believers. By now Mecca was hostile to Medina and launched a series of unsuccessful raids on the city. Muhammad was a skilled military leader who not only resisted attack but led an armed force of his own on Mecca in 630CE to cleanse the city of its pagan worship.

ART AT THE TIME OF SULEIMAN THE MAGNIFICENT

In the reign of the Ottoman Sultan, Suleiman the Magnificent (1520–1566CE), Islamic art and science flourished. At its height, the Ottoman Empire was one of the most influential in world history. The empire lasted until the end of World War I. Its capital, Constantinople (now Istanbul), was the centre of Islamic thought and produced a culture that embraced everything from ceramics and calligraphy, to architecture and astronomy. This mosque lamp of the period is characteristically ornate and comes from one of the numerous mosques that were constructed during Suleiman the Magnificent's reign.

Above This battle scene is from the 16th-century Book of Conquests by Suleiman. All Muslims are expected to defend Islam against outside threat by means of Jihad, or holy war. This also refers to a person's inner struggle against sin and temptation.

Muhammad's army met little resistance and he was able to take Mecca virtually without bloodshed. Many people who were initially hostile to Islam now embraced it and became Muslims themselves. One of the Prophet Muhammad's first tasks was to cleanse the Ka'ba (*see page 10*), of its idols and to return it to its original purity as a focal point for worship of the One God. To this day it remains Islam's holiest site.

Expansion

When the Prophet died in 632CE there was disagreement over who should succeed him – a disagreement that later resulted in the division between the Sunni and Shi'a branches of Islam. Muhammad's successor was his father-in-law, Abu Bakr, who became the caliph (*khalifa*), or head of state. Under the first four caliphs, Islam expanded at a colossal rate into present-day Egypt, Syria, Iraq and Iran.

After the caliphs the Umayyad dynasty (661–750CE) took the faith west as far as Spain and Morocco and east as far as India. Their successors, the Abbasids (750–1258CE), made Baghdad (in present-day Iraq) their capital and extended their territory still further into central Asia. In 1258, the Mongols took control of Baghdad and became Muslims themselves. In 1453, Constantinople (the Christian capital of the Byzantine Empire) fell to the Ottoman Turks and was eventually renamed Istanbul. Islam experienced another period of renewal in 1979, when the Iranian Revolution deposed the ruling monarch, the Shah of Iran, and introduced an Islamic state under the leadership of Ayatollah Khomeini.

THE LIFE OF THE PROPHET

Muhammad was born 570CE in the Arabian city of Mecca and was orphaned at the age of six. He was raised first by his grandfather, then by an uncle.

Early life

When Muhammad was a young man he went to work for a rich widow, Khadijah, whose camels and caravans he looked after. The city of Mecca was home to the Ka'ba, the 'sacred house' said to have been built by Abraham and his son Ishmael. In Muhammad's time it was filled with pagan idols worshipped by Arabian tribes who visited Mecca on pilgrimage. The merchants were happy with this arrangement because the pilgrims were a source of income. When he was 25, Muhammad married Khadijah and had several children by her. He became rich and highly respected in the city, but was uneasy with the pagan worship around him and sought solitude in the deserts and mountains.

Above The Dome of the Rock in Jerusalem houses the rock from which it is said that Muhammad ascended into Heaven.

The message from God

Aged 40, Muhammad was meditating in a cave outside Mecca when the Angel Jibril appeared. Jibril ordered Muhammad to read but when he replied that he could not, the Angel squeezed him tightly and insisted. 'Read', he said, 'read in the name of your Lord who created you from a drop of blood'. This was the first message that he received directly from Allah.

Left The Prophet's cave at Jebel Nur in present-day Saudi Arabia. Some Muslims believe this is where Adam, the first man created by Allah, appeared on Earth.

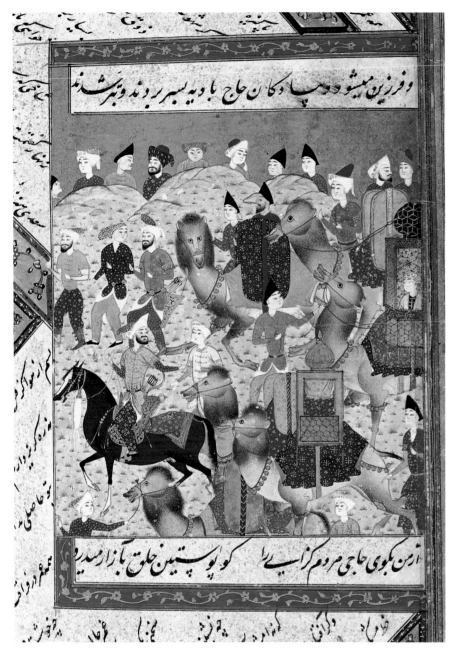

وفوزین میشو دپاد کان حاج با دید یسبررد ند ویرشد نی

ازین بکوی حاجی مردم کزا سیلرا   کو ایوستین خلق یا ز ازمیدر

Above *This print shows a caravan of pilgrims on the road to Mecca. In the past Muslims from all over the world travelled by foot, on horseback or camel. The journey could take years, so the pilgrims met many people along the way. Nowadays modern air travel means that Mecca is only hours away.*

> 'Be steadfast in prayer. Practise regular charity and bow down your heads with those who bow down in worship.'
>
> The Koran 2:43

The Night Journey

In about the tenth year of his ministry, Muhammad is said to have undergone a miraculous experience. In what has come to be called the Night Journey, he is said to have been taken up into the sky in the company of the angels. From Mecca he was taken to Jerusalem, where he prayed with the earlier prophets including Abraham, Moses and Jesus. After this, from a rock now contained in the Dome of the Rock in Jerusalem, he is believed to have ascended to heaven into the presence of Allah Himself, who told him to institute prayers five times a day.

The message spreads

Forced out of Mecca by persecution, Muhammad became the ruler of Medina, which was the target of hostilities by the people of Mecca. When Muhammad took Mecca in 630CE, he behaved with such generosity and tolerance that many of his former enemies became Muslims themselves. Two years after he had cleansed the Ka'ba of its pagan worship and restored it to the one God, Muhammad gave his last sermon to the people and declared that his aim in life was complete – he had delivered the word of Allah, which would remain true for all time. At the age of 63, Muhammad died in Medina, where he was buried.

THE KORAN

The Koran is the holy book of the Muslim world. The word means 'reading' and is taken from the instruction the Angel Jibril gave Muhammad (*see* page 10), that he should read the word of God.

Learning by heart

Because the revelation was in Arabic, Muslims have always studied the Koran in its original language. Very often, for boys and girls starting out on study, this means reciting the words while not fully understanding what they mean. However, since the words are believed to be the actual words of Allah, merely reciting them is seen as an act of worship in itself. Students are encouraged to learn as much of the Koran as they can by heart and in 1998 a six-year-old Muslim girl in South Africa became the youngest girl ever to have memorized the whole text in Arabic – 114 *suras* (chapters) in all, divided into verses.

Reverence for the holy book

The text is treated with great care and touched only by those who have ritually cleansed themselves beforehand. It is often wrapped in ornate cloth and kept in a special place in the home or mosque. Unlike the Ten Commandments, the Koran was not handed over at one single event in history, but over a period of 23 years. As a result it contains different styles of writing that deal with all aspects of life. There are instructions on how to pray, how to organize society and how to apply the law. It lists rules for the structure of family life, the duties of individuals to behave well, and penalties for sinners on Judgement Day. Above all, it stresses the 'Oneness' of Allah and the need to obey Him.

Above As an act of personal devotion, Muslim calligraphers (scribes who practise the art of handwriting) try to produce the most beautiful and ornate versions of the text by hand. This script with floral illuminations was written by Ismail Al-Zuhdi in 1802.

Left This boy is studying the Koran in Arabic at the Islamic School in London. In the Indian and Pakistani tradition, pupils sit round the edge of the schoolroom, not in rows behind each other. This is because it is considered disrespectful to have one's back to the Holy Book.

Other sources of guidance

Because Muhammad is believed to have led an exemplary life, his actions and sayings are considered to be of importance to Muslims. Stories of the Prophet's life are taken as practical examples of how devout Muslims should try to lead their own lives. Consequently, the traditional customs and practices of the Prophet (the *Sunna*) and his words and sayings (the *Haddith*) are consulted alongside the Koran and, with it, provide the faithful with a complete guide book to a godly life.

Although there are divisions within Islam and scholars from different traditions around the world may interpret the text in different ways, all Muslims accept the ultimate authority of the Koran over their lives and try to live by its rules.

> 'This is the Book. In it is guidance sure, without doubt to those who fear God.'
>
> The Koran 2:2

Below Some Muslims believe that the original version of the Koran has existed since the beginning of time on tablets stored in heaven. The text is venerated as the complete revelation of Allah's holy word.

MECCA AND THE FIVE PILLARS OF ISLAM

Mecca, the birthplace of the Prophet Muhammad, is a holy city and a place of pilgrimage for over two million Muslims every year. The pilgrimage, which all healthy Muslim men and women are expected to make at least once in a lifetime, is known as the *Hajj* and is the fifth of the 'Pillars of Islam'.

The *shahada*
Just as the pillars in a mosque support the building that rises above them, so the Pillars of Islam support the beliefs and practices of the Islamic faith. The first pillar is the statement of faith – the *shahada*.

Below At the centre of the holy city of Mecca is the Ka'ba, a cube-shaped shrine covered in black and gold velvet. When Muslim pilgrims visit the Ka'ba, they walk round it seven times in an anti-clockwise direction reciting prayers to Allah.

Left Regular prayer is central to Islamic practice. The women and children worship apart from the men.

It says, 'There is no god but Allah and Muhammad is the Messenger of Allah'. In reciting these words of faith, devout Muslims proclaim their belief in one God and their conviction that God's teaching has been revealed to Muhammad. This simple statement is the basis of all Muslim belief. It is the first thing whispered into a child's ear when he or she is born, and the last thing a Muslim hopes to utter at the moment of death.

Salat and zakat

The second pillar, *salat*, is daily worship – the prayers that are recited five times a day, at dawn, midday, afternoon, evening and night. Muslims stop what they are doing to bow down in worship in the direction of Mecca. The third pillar is *zakat*, or charitable giving. This has two functions. The first is to copy the generosity that Allah shows towards his people, and the second is to show kindness in a practical way to those less well off.

> **'I bear witness that there is no God but Allah and I bear witness that Muhammad is the messenger of Allah.'**
>
> Words from the *shahada*

Sawm

The fourth pillar is fasting, or *sawm*, which involves going without food and drink during daylight hours throughout the holy month of Ramadan. For people with jobs, and children who have school to attend, total abstinence is not easy, but it does bring spiritual reward. The end of Ramadan is celebrated with the festival of Eid ul-Fitr when presents are exchanged.

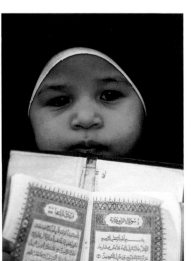

Left The religious duties of which the Five Pillars are the core are taught to Muslims such as this Algerian girl at an early age.

15

HEAVEN AND HELL

Muslims believe that while death is the end of earthly life it is the beginning of eternal life. They believe that faithfulness to Allah in this life will be rewarded in the next and that wickedness will be punished.

Angels and messengers

God is everywhere in Creation but cannot be seen. However, at points in human history it is believed that God sent special people to bring important spiritual messages. The first of these is said to be Adam, the first man, and the last was Muhammad, the 'Seal of the Prophets'. In addition, Muslims recognize the prophets of Judaism and Christianity including Noah, Abraham, Moses and Jesus.

Messengers are human but angels are not. The Koran says that they are winged creatures of light praising Allah and doing his will at all times. It is believed that all our deeds are being constantly recorded by them and that the angels will accompany human beings after death on the Day of Judgement.

Above *The righteous sit forever in the presence of God in this vision of Paradise. Heaven is shown here as a garden.*

Below *Iraqi Muslims carry a coffin across a mosque courtyard in Karbala. The body will be taken to its final earthly resting place, which faces the direction of Mecca.*

Death and judgement

Muslims about to die say the *shahada*, the profession of faith in one God and belief in his final prophet, Muhammad. It was the first thing they heard when they came into the world and it is the last thing they say before they leave it.

The dead are buried as soon as possible. After the body has been washed it is wrapped in a shroud and treated with great reverence as if the person were still alive. For this reason Islam forbids cremation. The body is placed in the grave (with its head facing Mecca) where it will wait until the Last Day when, it is believed, the dead will rise and be judged.

Heaven

Heaven is the eternal reward for those who have followed the will of Allah. Heaven is described in the Koran as a beautiful garden where the righteous can eat fruits and drink juices while reclining on comfortable couches and waited on by heavenly servants. Those who have led a good life are admitted to Paradise after they have been judged by the Almighty. Martyrs, who have died for their faith, are said to proceed straight to Heaven without the need to account for their earthly lives to the angels and to God.

Some interpret this literally while others say it is an image describing the joy of being eternally in God's presence.

Above In this vision of Hell a sinner is consumed by flames of unquenchable fire. The souls of those already damned are pressed tightly together (bottom left) to be tortured throughout eternity.

Hell

Hell, by contrast, is an ugly place reserved for the wicked and the unbelievers. It is described as a place of everlasting fire, boiling waters, scorching winds and black smoke.

The punishments of Hell are believed to be eternal and the sinners' bodies are eternally renewed so that the torments can continue for ever. Although they are described as physical tortures, many Islamic scholars argue that they are dramatic images that powerfully describe the pain of separation from God.

ISLAMIC LAW AND SCIENCE

The system of Islamic law known as *Shari'a* comes from the Arabic word describing a track leading camels to a watering-hole – a description implying a pathway that, if followed by humanity, will lead to Allah.

Above *Islamic law deals with all aspects of family life. A man may have more than one wife, provided he can look after them equally – an arrangement that is, however, increasingly rare in the West.*

Sources of the law

The Koran and the *Sunna* (customs and practices of the Prophet) are the two principal sources of the law in Islam. There are five categories of action: what Allah has decreed, what Allah has forbidden, what Allah has recommended but not insisted on, what Allah has disapproved of but not expressly forbidden and what Allah has remained silent about. An example of these distinctions is contained in Islam's attitude to alcohol and tobacco. The consumption of alcohol – an intoxicant – is definitely forbidden, but tobacco is different. Some scholars have argued that it is not covered in the Koran, although they suspect it is a grey area that, while not expressly forbidden, is disapproved of. As a result, Muslims may smoke pipes or cigarettes and still be within the law.

Interpreting the law

Shari'a deals with every aspect of human society including family life, property, crime, punishment, business and morality. In practice it has been supplemented with legislation adapted to suit the needs of different communities. Scholars constantly interpret the law, and their findings also become a basis for law-making. Experts able to rule on points of law are known as *muftis*. Shi'a Muslims also accept the rulings of their highest religious leaders, the ayatollahs. Interpretation of Islamic law may vary, but its fundamentals will always apply.

Right *Young women working in the laboratory in Egypt continue the centuries-old tradition of scholarship and science.*

Above This painting shows astronomers at work in the 16th-century observatory in Istanbul. Globes, maps, astrolabes, telescopes and compasses have all been refined by Muslim scientists.

'It is God who sends the winds and they raise the clouds. Then does He spread them in the sky as He wills.'

The Koran 30:48

Muslim scholarship

Throughout the Dark Ages of Europe (c.500–1100CE) the flame of scholarship was kept alive by writers, philosophers and mathematicians from the Islamic world, who translated many of the classical texts of ancient Greece into Arabic. The western system of numerals is of Arabic origin. By superseding Roman numerals, they made modern mathematics possible. Muslim mathematicians also gave the world algebra.

Astronomical exploration

Islamic scientists founded observatories from which they plotted the positions of the stars. They used and refined a special instrument known as an astrolabe, which enabled them to carry out a scientific function (measuring the angle of the stars and plotting distances and directions on the ground) and a religious function (establishing the direction of Mecca – the *qibla* – for their daily prayers). Astrolabes were important tools for navigation and map-making, and opened up the way for even more scientific discoveries. Islam, which has produced eminent philosophers, doctors and scientists, encourages scholarship, but it also teaches that Allah alone is the source of all knowledge and all creation.

THE MOSQUE

The word 'mosque' comes from an Arabic word that means 'place of prostration'. It is the house of prayer where Muslims gather together to worship Allah. There are many different styles of mosque, and they reflect the traditional architecture of the countries in which they are found. However, all of them share common design features.

Pointers to Allah

Perhaps the most distinctive element of a mosque is its minaret, the tall, slender tower designed to be seen from a distance as a reminder of Allah's presence. As one's gaze is taken up the minaret to the top, one is symbolically looking up towards heaven, where Allah is supreme. Similarly, the dome of the mosque symbolizes the roof of the sky where Allah reigns in splendour and majesty.

The harmony of creation

Although the mosque will often be richly ornamented, the decorations are always abstract and geometrical, symbolizing divine harmony. Because Muslims are anxious to avoid the sin of idolatry (worshipping anything other than the One God), there are never any pictures of people or animals that might accidentally distract the worshipper from Allah alone.

House of prayer

The mosque is usually full at midday on Friday, which is an important day for communal worship. Unlike Judaism and Christianity, Islam has no concept of the Sabbath. As Allah never stops working, Muslims believe that they should not stop working either.

Left Traditionally the muezzin *(or proclaimer) calls the faithful to prayer from the minaret or tower of the mosque. In most Islamic countries the task is now carried out electronically through a loudspeaker system.*

The *mihrab* is a niche in the wall that marks the direction of Mecca.

The *minbar* is a pulpit from which the *imam* delivers his sermon on Fridays.

The minarets have balconies from which the call to prayer is given by the *muezzin*.

Left *The Blue Mosque in Istanbul is one of the most beautiful religious buildings in the world. It was built between 1609 and 1616CE on the orders of Sultan Ahmet I.*

Once they have said Friday prayers, they resume their working day. Prayer is led by a religious leader (*imam*) or by a preacher (*khatib*). When praying, Muslims always face Mecca – the direction is indicated by an empty niche or alcove known as the *mihrab*. Because prayer involves ritual movements of standing, kneeling and bowing, the space in the main prayer hall has no seating of any kind. Instead carpets cover the floor, marking it out as holy ground. Although some mosques have a separate space for women to worship, mosque prayer is usually an all-male activity. Worshippers leave their shoes at the door and proceed to a small room – usually a communal space with low seats in front of individual taps – where they rinse their hands, face, nostrils, mouth, arms and feet in ritual purification.

Above *Men congregate for prayer at the Prophet's Mosque in Medina, Saudi Arabia. They kneel on carpets and face Mecca.*

The fountain in the courtyard was used for ritual ablutions. These are now carried out under taps outside walls of the mosque.

Equality in the sight of Allah

In the prayer hall the worshippers line up together – young, old, rich and poor occupying the same space to show that all are equal in the sight of Allah. Next to the *mihrab* is the *minbar*, resembling a small staircase, from which the preacher delivers his sermon, or *khutba*. Mosque worship is based on the word of Allah so there is no singing or music of any kind. Muslims believe that corporate worship is more pleasing to Allah than individual prayer, so they make a special effort to attend.

ISLAMIC ART

Muslims believe in one indivisible God and are taught to avoid the worship of false gods and idols. As a result, many are suspicious of paintings and statues representing human forms – for fear they could accidentally be worshipped as pagan idols. However, there is a tradition of representational art, often showing imagined scenes from Islamic history, but this is never incorporated into mosque design or seen in places of worship.

Calligraphy and the decorative arts

Calligraphy, or the art of handwriting, is an art form prized highly in the Islamic world. It is believed that the word of God is so important that it must be written down with reverence and in the most beautiful ways possible. Calligraphers through the generations have produced elaborate editions of the holy texts and used all their skills to shape and colour each Arabic character with the utmost care.

Concern with beauty is seen as a mark of respect for the Almighty and, in their small way, finely decorated objects such as mosaics, ceramics, carpets and pieces of metalwork, are seen to mirror the beauty of God's Creation.

In contrast to the western tradition, which has emphasised painting and sculpture, Islam has tended to focus on what are called the decorative arts – producing exquisitely designed domestic objects such as tapestries, glassware, pottery, plates and lamps.

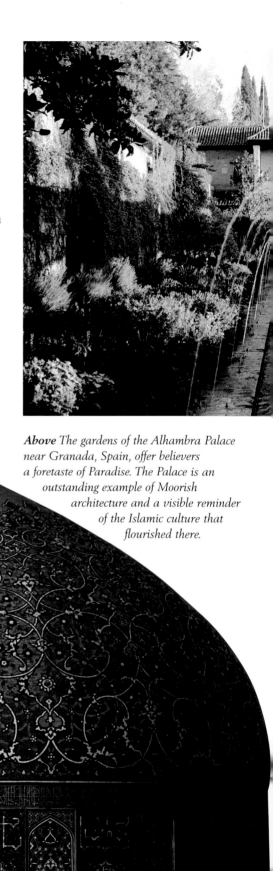

Above The gardens of the Alhambra Palace near Granada, Spain, offer believers a foretaste of Paradise. The Palace is an outstanding example of Moorish architecture and a visible reminder of the Islamic culture that flourished there.

Right Intricate patterns and repeating geometric shapes decorate the dome of the Sheikh Lutfullah Mosque in Isfahan, Iran. They signify the immensity of Creation.

Below The Great Mosque in Cordoba, southern Spain, was begun in 785CE. The Mosque shows how art and architecture can help to inspire worshippers.

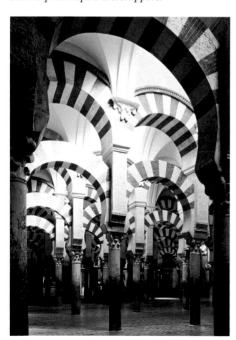

The Ottomans

The empire of the Ottoman Turks lasted for nearly 500 years from the mid-15th century CE. It reached its height during the reign of Suleiman the Magnificent (1520-1566CE). His empire stretched from the north African coast through the Balkans to the gates of Vienna and was seen as his reward for spreading the faith of Islam so effectively.

Under his rule, an elaborate artistic tradition evolved with artists and craftspeople producing magnificent ornaments decorated with valuable materials such as gold, silver and precious stones. During Suleiman's time, great mosques were constructed and survive today as some of the most magnificent in the world.

Left The Prophet Muhammad rides ahead of his disciples to meet the enemy army from Mecca.

Islamic gardens

Islamic gardens are designed and built to represent Heaven on earth. They first emerged in the dusty desert plains of Persia and served as beautiful spaces set apart from the harshness of the surrounding landscape where people could read, relax and experience some of the beauty of Allah's Creation.

They were planted with beautifully coloured flowers and fruit trees bearing lemons, dates, figs, pomegranates, as well as vines for grapes. Water is a constant feature of the Islamic garden and channels traditionally divide the space into four sections – in the same way that the Garden of Eden is said to have been fed and divided by two rivers.

But the water is not just symbolically important. It is a cooling element in the garden producing pleasing reflections and soothing sounds. In the baking summer heat the garden with its water, light, shade and colour gives believers a foretaste of the life to come in Paradise.

WORSHIP AND FESTIVALS

Muslims believe that humans were created to worship God and the purpose of life itself is total submission to His will. *Salat*, the set prayers that are recited five times a day in the direction of Mecca, give a structure to the day. Muslims will often have a special prayer rug, or *sajjada*, for use in the home or when they are travelling. This allows them to create a ritually pure and holy space from which to direct their thoughts to Allah. In the home and in the mosque shoes are removed as a sign of reverence.

The festival year

Just as prayers punctuate the day, so do festivals punctuate the Islamic year, which has 12 lunar months, or 354 days. In some Islamic traditions the calendar begins with the celebration of the *hijra*, the Prophet's migration from Mecca to Medina in 622CE. This is followed two months later by a festival marking his birthday in 570CE.

The ninth month of Ramadan is the most significant of the year and it is marked by a complete abstinence from food and drink during the hours of daylight. It is believed that the Prophet received Allah's first revelation during Ramadan and as a result it is kept holy. Fasting is a physical and spiritual discipline designed to focus attention on Allah in a concentrated way and it is a duty that every fit and healthy adult is expected to perform. Children are not expected to fast, but many do so in imitation of their parents' devotion to Allah.

Above *Five times a day Muslims stop whatever they are doing, face the direction of Mecca and prostrate themselves in prayer.*

Left *These children have a homemade Eid card. The end of Ramadan is associated with blessings and joy, and people often exchange presents.*

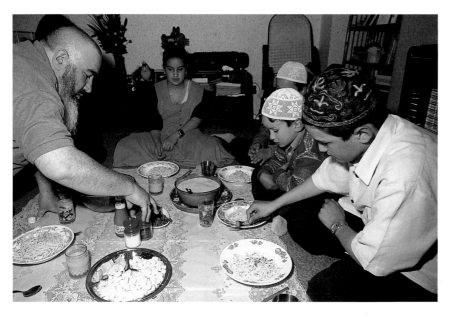

Above Ramadan ends with the joyful
festival of Eid ul-Fitr, when families and
friends break their month-long fast.

> ‘People, adore your
> Guardian – Lord who
> created you.’
>
> The Koran 2:21

Daily routine

In many households the day
begins before dawn with prayers
and a reading from the Koran.
People then set off for work,
school or college knowing that
they will not be able to eat or
drink anything until the Sun has
set. Attendance at the mosque
increases during Ramadan,
particularly towards the end
of the month when people gather to commemorate *Lailat al-Qadr*,
the Night of Power, when it is believed Allah first revealed His holy
law to the Prophet Muhammad. Muslims try to stay awake all
night and may remain in the mosque praying or reciting from the
Koran. The fast concentrates mind, body and spirit on Allah and
demonstrates that it is important to resist temptation.
It is also thought to be a way for the rich
to experience the hardship of the poor.

Fasting for a feast

Ramadan ends as soon as the new Moon
is sighted – in some Muslim countries
this is signalled by the sound of a
cannon. The fasting stops and Muslims
prepare for the joyful festival of Eid ul-
Fitr, when they sit down to enjoy their
first meal during daylight for a month.
Richer families are expected to give
food to the poor so that everyone can
mark the day happily. Often presents
are exchanged, symbolizing the
blessings and happiness that await
all those who follow Allah’s will.

Left Children from Singapore celebrate the
end of Ramadan. People put on their best
clothes to celebrate the day in style.

25

ISLAMIC CUSTOMS

Islam attaches great importance to family life and sees the family as a small-scale model of the perfect society that God has planned for his Creation. In this society-in-miniature the strong take care of the weak, the old pass on their knowledge and experience to the young and each treats the other with respect. Children are particularly important members of the family unit. They are vulnerable and trusting and so should be treated lovingly by their parents who are responsible for setting a good example in their religious life. In return, children are expected to obey their parents in all things lawful and take care of them in their old age.

Marriage and divorce

In Islam, marriage is the basis of family life and the only place for the physical expression of love between a man and a woman. Although it is increasingly rare in the West, a man is allowed to have up to four wives – provided that he is able to support them all financially and is prepared to treat each of them equally.

Islam, however, also recognizes that marriages can sometimes break down and divorce is permitted if both partners have tried unsuccessfully to resolve their marital problems. Even so, divorce is always a matter of great sadness and regret and the Prophet Muhammad expressed his sorrow at the reality of marital breakdown.

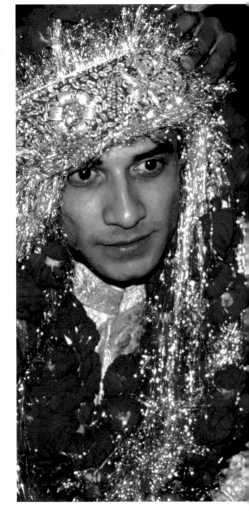

Above *A Muslim marriage is a joyful event for the families as well as for the community. This Iranian couple are at the centre of celebrations.*

Left *These Muslim girls are studying a religious text in a mosque in Germany. In addition to such subjects as maths, science, history and geography, Islam lays great stress on religious education.*

Right Family life is an important part of Islam. These Malaysian parents can offer the physical care and spiritual guidance their child needs.

The community

Muslims are expected to fulfil their duties within the family but also to serve the wider community. Those who are able are expected, every year, to give 2.5 per cent of what they have (after they have met their own needs) to the poor and the needy.

Charitable giving (*zakat*) does not always involve money and in certain countries may take the form of crops, cattle, gold or precious stones. Islam sees the world as a place where all human beings are interdependent and the role of the community is extremely important. The community exists to celebrate life in times of joy and to support people in times of hardship.

The money raised or donated by people will often be spent on building mosques or community centres serving both the material and spiritual needs of ordinary Muslims.

Education

Islam has always prized learning and education. In Muslim countries there is no division between secular and religious education. All subjects are taught within the framework of the Islamic faith. In the West, Muslim boys and girls are taught general subjects such as maths, history, geography and science, but their parents also hope that they will receive a thorough grounding in the principles of the faith. Others say that religious education is best left to the parents and the mosque.

Above Islam takes its responsibility to the wider community very seriously. The Red Crescent is a religious charity that offers help to those affected by hunger and disease throughout the world.

DIVISION AND DIVERSITY

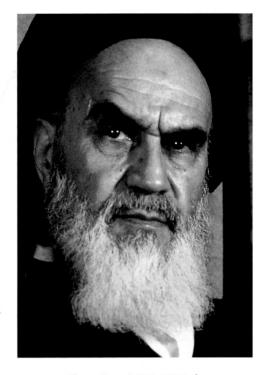

The Koran describes Muhammad as the 'Seal of the Prophets', that is to say, with him the line of the prophets (beginning with Adam and continuing through Abraham, Moses and Jesus) has been sealed for all time. Muhammad is the last and no other will follow him.

After the Prophet
Problems arose after the Prophet's death when there was disagreement about who should lead the Muslim community. Two branches, Sunni and Shi'a, emerged. The Sunnis took their name from the *Sunna*, or traditions of the Prophet. They argued that as no one could ever equal Muhammad in wisdom and goodness, his chosen successor had to be the person judged most suitable by the community. The Prophet's first successor was Abu Bakr, who became the first of the four caliphs who ruled the (as yet) undivided *umma*, or community of believers.

The decisive split
The group who were eventually to become the Shi'as were unhappy with this arrangement and argued that only Muhammad's nearest relative, his cousin and son-in-law Ali, was fit to follow in the Prophet's footsteps. Becoming known as the 'followers of the party of Ali' or 'shi'at Ali' (Shi'a for short), they believed that Ali had inherited some of the qualities and authority of their founder, qualities that made him especially suitable to become their religious leader, or *imam*. The decisive split between Sunnis and Shi'as came in 680CE, when Ali's son Hussain was killed by Muslim rivals at the Battle of Karbala. His tomb, in what is now southern Iraq, is still regarded as one of the holiest shrines in the Shi'a Islamic world.

Above From 1979–1989 the influence of Ayatollah Khomeini was important in defining the character of Shi'a Islam. The revolution he inspired in Iran, and his insistence on a particular type of Islamic purity, brought him into direct conflict with countries in the West.

Right These Chinese children reciting parts of the Koran in Arabic show how far Islam has travelled from its beginnings on the Arabian Peninsula.

Above *Islamic dress should be modest at*
all times, but different countries interpret
modesty differently. These Afghanistan
women wear a very conservative style of
dress that leaves only the eyes visible, and
these are also sometimes covered by a veil.

Shi'as and Sunnis

Shiism itself soon divided, this time into three groups. The majority Imami, or Twelver, group, found mostly in Iran, Iraq and Lebanon, believed in 12 principal *imams*, the twelfth of whom is said to have disappeared, but will return at the end of time. The Ismailis, or Severner, group supported a man named Ismail as the seventh *Imam* in his claim to be the head of Shiism. The Ziadis, the third group, are found mostly in Yemen. Sunni Muslims account for some 90 per cent of the world's Islamic population. A principal centre of Sunni Islam is Saudi Arabia, which is also guardian of the most important religious shrine in Mecca. Shi'a Muslims, most of whom live in Iran, account for the remaining 10 per cent.

> **'When you recite the Koran, seek refuge in God from accursed Satan.'**
>
> The Koran 16:98

THE WAY OF THE SUFI

The Sufis are not a separate branch of Islam. They can be drawn from both the Sunni and Shi'a groups and are defined by their mystical approach to the faith. Taking their name from the *suf* – the simple woollen robe they used to wear (*suf* means 'wool') – they search for a closer, personal relationship with Allah. Sufism was influenced by the ascetic practices (giving up material possessions) of Christian monks and hermits. Like them, Sufis turned their back on the world and took vows of poverty.

The mystical tradition

During a service known as a *dhikr*, Sufis use singing, dance and drumming to focus all their attention on Allah. In this state of heightened concentration on the divine presence, they hope to forget themselves and the everyday world completely so that their soul can be free to unite with Allah Himself. The Sufi tradition produced the most famous female mystic in Islam's history: Rabi'a al-Adawiyya (721–801CE) was a slave girl who devoted her life entirely to Allah.

Closer communion with God

In the 12th century CE, a number of Sufi orders or brotherhoods (*tariqas*) sprang up and were based in enclosed communities set aside for study and prayer. Perhaps the best known of the Sufi groups that the *tariqas* produced are the Dervishes, whose name comes from the Turkish and Persian words meaning 'beggar'. They, too, took vows of poverty and devoted their lives to union with Allah. Following the guidance of a religious teacher (a *shaykh* or *pir*), they practise rituals that induce an almost hypnotic or trance-like state in which they hope to come into a closer union with Allah.

Left *This woman uses prayer beads to aid her devotion. They are a physical way of helping the mind to focus on Allah.*

Above Whirling Dervishes of the Turkish Sufi sect spin round to induce a trance-like state which, it is believed, brings them into a closer relationship with Allah.

The Whirling Dervishes

Unlike other Muslim groups, the Sufis use ritual music in their devotions. The group popularly called the Whirling Dervishes rotate round and round to the accompaniment of a repetitive beat, seeking a higher level of consciousness that they hope will ultimately bring them into direct contact with Allah. The whirling is said to imitate the rotation of the planets round the Sun and that of the whole of creation round Allah. For some Muslims, music is considered ungodly because it can lead to temptation, but for Sufis it is often used as an actual aid to devotion. Sufi mysticism appeals as much to the heart as to the head, and at its centre is the simple but all-consuming love of Allah.

POLITICAL ISLAM

Islam is not just a religion. It is a complete and interconnecting system of thought and practice that influences every aspect of social, political, economic, cultural and spiritual life.

The Islamic state

Throughout the history of Islam, people have tried to create a society in keeping with God's eternal laws as revealed in the Koran and explained by the Prophet. The ideal has been an Islamic state – a society ruled by Shari'a, or religious law, which, in turn, is interpreted by the religious scholars. This means that clergymen govern the state rather than secular politicians elected by the people.

The religious authorities rule on everything from how people should dress to the severity of punishments for breaking the law.

The modern dilemma

The problem facing Muslim countries in the 21st century is whether they should impose a completely Islamic way of life on their people or whether they should incorporate the liberal, democratic principles of the Western world into their own societies.

Some Muslim scholars argue that only by keeping totally separate from western values can the purity of Islam survive. Others argue that Muslim societies, too, can enjoy the benefits of new technology, for example, while remaining true to their faith.

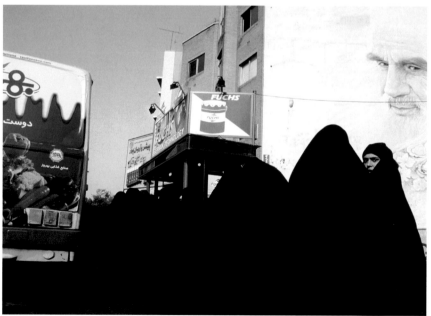

Right Women wait at a bus stop in Tehran under the eyes of Ayatollah Khomeini (1900-1989) who transformed Iran into an Islamic republic following a popular uprising in 1979.

Fundamentalism

Muslim fundamentalism is an attempt to revive what it sees as the authentic faith of Islam undiluted by western secular values. It claims that both socialism and capitalism have failed to create prosperous and just societies for Muslim people, leaving them materially and spiritually worse off. Using the Koran as their authority (and often interpreting it literally) Islamic fundamentalists challenge the values of liberal democracies head-on and seek to impose (sometimes by persuasion and sometimes by force) what they consider is the only true form of Islam.

The most extreme form of fundamentalism in recent times was found in Afghanistan at the end of the 20th century under the ruling Taliban. Television, music and radio were banned, women were forced to cover themselves from head to foot and denied education, and a strict system of punishments was introduced for breaches of the religious law. The rule came to an end after an American-led invasion in 2001, but groups of Taliban supporters still operate in the country and are believed to encourage global terrorism.

Above *The Blue Mosque dominates the skyline of Istanbul. Although Turkey's population is predominantly Muslim, its constitution is secular and rule is by elected politicians, not by the clergy.*

Right *Islamist militants believe that their interpretation of the Koran is, broadly speaking, the only genuine one. For them this sometimes justifies violence in the pursuit of what they see as a religious duty.*

The Turkish model

In 1923, Turkey became the first Islamic country to declare itself a secular state. Although men and women are free to worship there are restrictions on the way they can practise their faith in public life. Government is by elected politicians not by the clergy and Turkish society is heavily influenced by Western culture.

However, the widespread support for the traditions of Islam means that there is tension between those who want to see religion in political life and those who do not.

Many People – One Faith

Islam has been compared to a river of clear water taking on different colours as it flows over the different landscapes of the world. In other words, the faith of Islam remains the same even though local, regional and national variations in each particular culture lend it an outwardly different appearance.

Many models of Islam

Some countries, such as Iran under the late Ayatollah Khomeini, strongly resisted secular Western influence in order to create a strictly Islamic society governed by the clergy. Others, for example Turkey and some north African countries, have attempted to separate religion and politics and have embraced Western ideas. By contrast, the desert kingdom of Saudi Arabia practises an austere form of Islam, sometimes known as *Wahabism*, and has religious police to enforce mosque attendance, modest dress and Islamic behaviour at all times.

Above The Muslim community has spread out beyond its birthplace in the Arabian desert and is now equally at home in the cities of Europe and America.

Although Islam is often associated with the Arab culture of the Middle East, countries including Malaysia and Indonesia (the largest Muslim nation in the world) have evolved unique cultures of their own owing little to the Arab influence. Islamic law exists but it is largely confined to family and domestic issues.

Islam in the West

For Muslims living in countries where the dominant culture is non-Islamic there are both opportunities and challenges. Europe's growing Islamic community, for example, is exploring ways of being both fully European and fully Muslim. They are working out ways of integrating with mainstream society while at the same time holding true to the core beliefs of their faith.

Right Although the faith of Islam is universal it boasts a variety of different cultural expressions. Here, a Muslim man prays amid the distinctive mud architecture of sub-Saharan Africa.

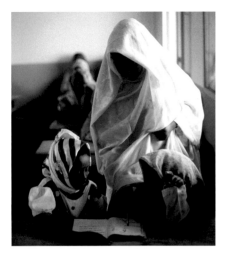

Above A Muslim woman supervises children at a Muslim school. Today, growing numbers of Muslim women, especially in the West, are encouraged to study and find work.

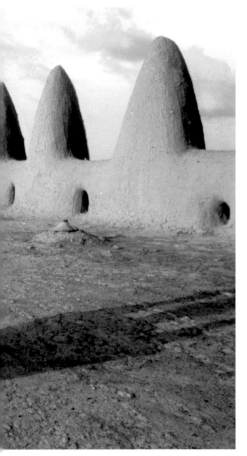

Cultural misunderstandings can arise when teachers and religious leaders (*imams*) are imported from abroad. They may bring with them practices that are culturally bound to remote rural areas – sometimes these practices are inappropriate to modern Western city life. Increasingly, *imams* are being trained within the communities they serve so that they are familiar with the demands of Western societies. The challenge for Muslims in Manchester or London, for example, is to fashion a form of Islam which enables them to say, 'We are both British and Muslim at the same time'.

The future

In recent times, Islam has undergone a revival among its estimated one billion followers worldwide. Some conservative scholars look to past traditions to forge what they believe is a pure and authentic version of the faith. Others, however, have argued that the faith has to be reformed to suit the needs of the 21st century. While remaining faithful to the message of Islam, they say that the meaning of the Koran has to be constantly studied and reinterpreted for each successive generation.

Even so, all devout Muslims agree that the message of Allah is valid for all time and for all people in all countries and that He has revealed His purpose for Creation in the Holy Koran and in the teachings of the Prophet Muhammad. By faithful submission to God's laws they believe that they will enjoy not only a full and good life on Earth but, after death, an eternity of bliss in the presence of the Almighty Himself.

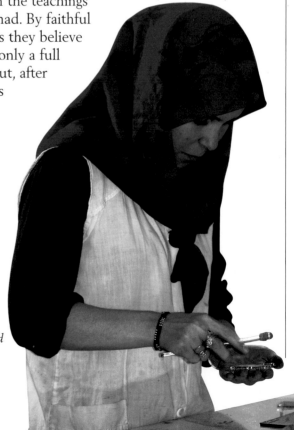

Right Although the core message of Islam is unchanging, traditions vary from country to country. This Algerian woman, for example, is not required to wear the full body covering worn by many Middle Eastern women. Instead the traditional Muslim headscarf or 'hijab' is recognized as appropriately modest dress.

GLOSSARY

Allah God.

Angel A supernatural winged being serving God.

Ayatollah A senior Shi'a leader.

Calligraphy The art of handwriting.

Day of Judgement The day, after death, when our earthly lives will be judged by God.

Dhikr A Sufi service.

Eid ul-Fitr The celebration ending the fast of the holy month of Ramadan.

Eternal life Everlasting life which follows this earthly life.

Fast Abstaining from food as part of a spiritual discipline.

Five Pillars of Islam The principal duties every Muslim must carry out.

Fundamentalism A strict, often literal, interpretation of religious teaching.

Haddith The sayings of the Prophet.

Hajj The pilgrimage to Mecca, and the fifth Pillar of Islam.

Halal That which is allowed.

Haram That which is forbidden.

Heaven The place of eternal joy reserved for those who have followed God's laws.

Hell The place of eternal torment reserved for sinners after death.

Hijab A Muslim headscarf.

Hijra The Prophet's migration from Mecca to Medina.

Hilal The crescent moon.

Idol A stone or wooden statue to a god or gods.

Illuminated Elaborately handwritten texts.

Imam An Islamic religious leader.

Integration Becoming a part of mainstream society rather than living apart from it.

Islamic state A political system based on the laws of God.

Jihad The personal and internal struggle with oneself to be godly. Also a holy war in defence of Islam.

Judgement A decision or sentence handed down, especially by God.

Khatib A Muslim preacher.

Khutba A sermon or public speech.

Koran The Muslim holy book containing God's revelation.

Madrassa A Muslim religious academy.

Martyr Someone who is prepared to suffer or die for the faith.

Meditate To focus the mind on a spiritual subject.

Mihrab The niche in a mosque marking the direction of Mecca.

Minaret The distinctive tower of a mosque.

Minbar The pulpit from which the sermon is given.

Monotheism Belief in one God.

Moors The Muslim people of North Africa.

Mosque A Muslim place of worship.

Muezzin The man calling the faithful to prayer from the minaret of the mosque.

Mufti A religious scholar.

Mystical Referring to the religious tradition that seeks a closer personal experience of God.

Night Journey The Prophet's angelic journey across the sky from Mecca to Jerusalem, followed by his ascension into Heaven to meet Allah.

Pagan Relating to the worship of many gods.

Persecution Ill-treatment because of the religious beliefs one holds.

Pilgrimage A journey to a holy place.

Polytheism Belief in more than one god.

Prophet A person who proclaims the message of God.

Prostrate To lie or bend with face towards the ground (in submission to God).

Qibla The direction of Mecca.

Ramadan The holy month of fasting, when no food or drink is consumed during daytime.

Revelation The disclosure of God's purpose for Creation.

Righteous Good in the sight of God.

Sacred Holy.

Sajjada A prayer rug.

Salat Daily worship, the second of the Five Pillars of Islam.

Sawm Fasting, the fourth of the Five Pillars of Islam.

Sect A small group of people with religious beliefs different from the mainstream.

Secular Non-religious.

Shahada The profession of faith in one God, the first of the Five Pillars of Islam.

Shari'a The system of Islamic law, covering every aspect of society.

Shaykh (**Sheikh**) A religious scholar.

Shi'a A branch of Islam guided both by the traditions of the Prophet and by the wisdom of his descendants.

Shroud A sheet for wrapping dead bodies prior to burial.

Sinner Someone who breaks God's laws.

Sufism The mystical tradition of Islam.

Sultan A Muslim king or sovereign.

Sunna The customs and traditions of the Prophet, one of the two main sources of the law in Islam.

Sunni The largest branch of Islam, who take their name from the *Sunna* and are guided by the traditions of the Prophet.

Sura A verse in the Koran.

Tariqa A Sufi brotherhood.

Umma The community of Islamic believers.

Zakat Charitable giving, the third of the Five Pillars of Islam.

INDEX

ACKNOWLEDGEMENTS

The Publisher would like to thank the following for permission to reproduce their material. Every care has been taken to trace copyright holders. However, if there have been unintentional omissions or failure to trace copyright holders, we apologise and will, if informed, endeavour to make corrections in any future edition.

Cover main and inset Corbis; page 1 Getty; 6tr Peter Sanders; 7bl Sygma/ S. Elbaz; 7t Bridgeman Art Library/ British Museum; 8tr Hutchison Library/Mary Jelliffe; 8bl Michael Holford; 9 Sonia Halliday/ Topkapi Palace Museum, Istanbul; 10tr Sygma/A.Gyori; 10bl Peter Sanders; 11 Bridgeman Art Library/British Library; 12tr Bridgeman Art Library; 12bl Peter Sanders; 13 Bridgeman Art Library/Musee Conde, Chantilly; 14–15 Peter Sanders; 15tl Magnum Photos/Abbas; 15bc Frank Spooner; 16tr Art Archive; 16b Corbis; 17 Art Archive; 18tr Peter Sanders; 18br Magnum Photos/Abbas; 19 Sonia Halliday, Istanbul University Library; 20 bl Hutchison Library/Isabella Tree; 20–21 Roger Hutchins; 21tr Peter Sanders; 22–23t Alamy; 22b Corbis; 23tr Art Archive; 23bl Alamy; 24tr Format/ Impact; 24bl Trip/H. Rogers; 25tl Trip/H. Rogers; 25bl Trip; 26–27t Corbis; 26b Still Pictures; 27b Panos Pictures; 28tr Sygma/ Alain Dejean; 28br Impact/Mark Henley; 29t Magnum Photos/ Abbas; 30bl Peter Sanders; 30–31 Robert Harding; 32–33 Getty; 32b Corbis; 33br Corbis; 34tr Panos Pictures; 34–35b Still Pictures; 35tl Corbis; 35br Corbis